The Let's Talk Library™

Let's Talk About
Going to the Hospital

Marianne Johnston

The Rosen Publishing Group's
PowerKids Press™
New York

Published in 1997 by The Rosen Publishing Group, Inc.
29 East 21st Street, New York, NY 10010

First Edition

Book design: Erin McKenna

Photo credits: All photos by Seth Dinnerman.

Johnston, Marianne.
    Let's talk about going to the hospital / Marianne Johnston.
        p.   cm. — (The Let's talk library)
    Includes index.
    Summary: Explains what a hospital is, what happens there, and when a patient can go home.
    ISBN 0-8239-5036-0
    1. Hospitals—Juvenile literature. 2. Children—Preparation for medical care—Juvenile literature. [1. Hospitals. 2. Medical care.] I. Title. II. Series.
    RA963.5.J64 1996
    362.1'1—dc20
                                        96-27206
                                           CIP
                                         AC

Manufactured in the United States of America

Table of Contents

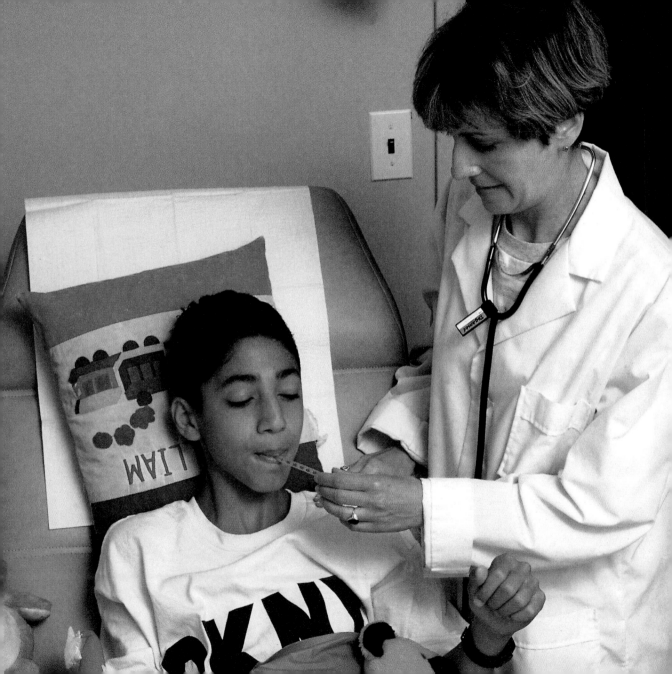

What Is a Hospital?

Sometimes we get sick or hurt. Usually a visit to the doctor and a few days in bed is enough to make us better. But sometimes we need more help to get healthy. We may have to go to the **hospital** (HOS-pih-tul) for a few days. A hospital is a place where doctors and nurses work. They take care of sick and hurt people. These people are called **patients** (PAY-shints). Doctors and nurses work hard to make patients **healthy** (HEL-thee).

◄ Hospitals are special places where people who are sick go to get well.

Hospitals Can Seem Scary

The hospital can be a scary place if you don't know what to expect. Most hospitals are really big. They have lots of hallways and rooms. Hospitals are full of busy doctors, nurses, and other workers. These people always seem to be in a hurry. But they're hurrying so that they can help more people.

The hospital may seem scary. But remember: It's a place filled with people who want to help you get well.

Going to a hospital may be scary, but your mom or dad will be there with you. ▶

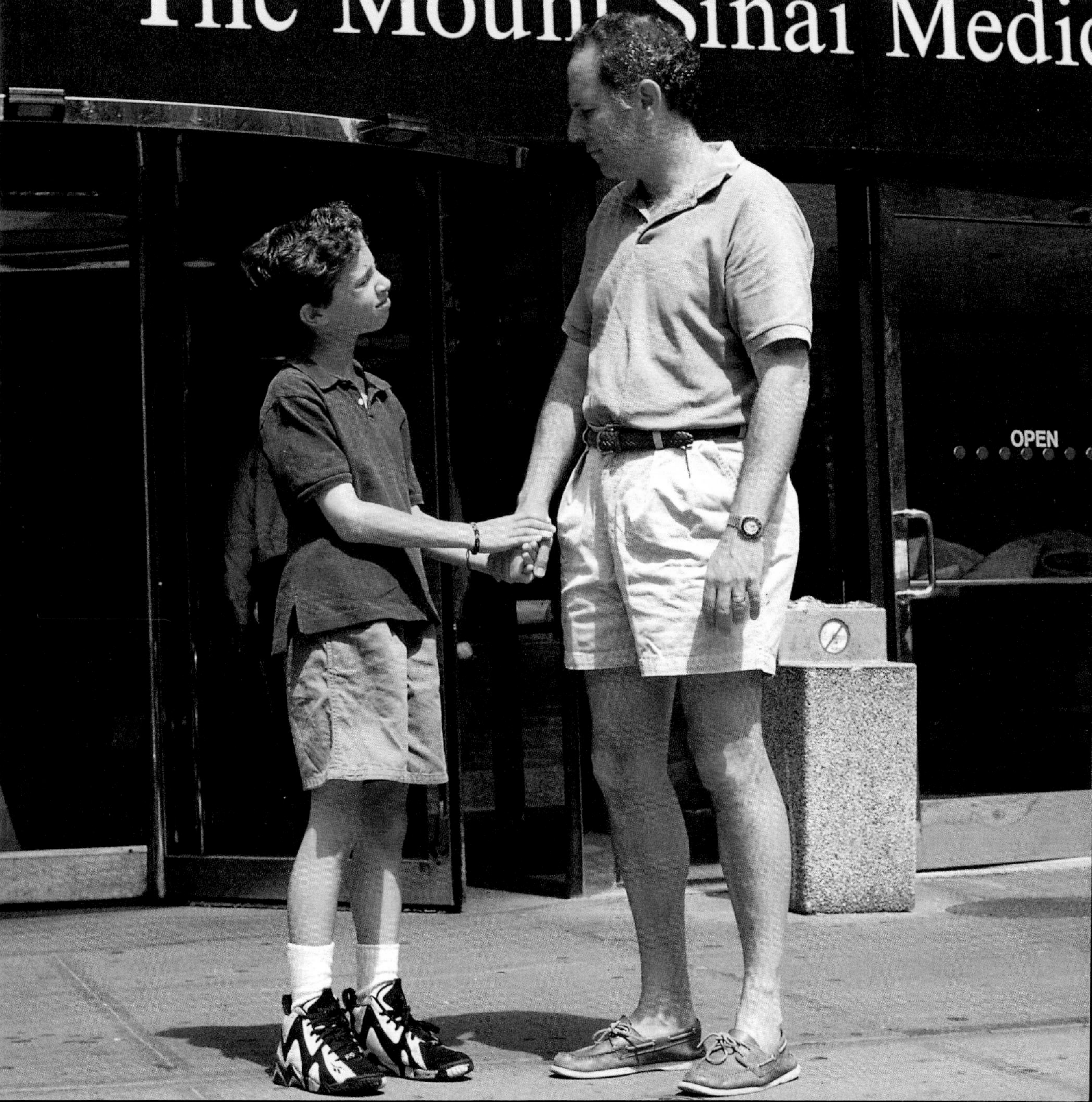
The Mount Sinai Medic
OPEN

What to Pack

Before you go to the hospital, you'll need to pack a few things. You'll need your toothbrush. You can also pack some of your toys and books. And you can take your favorite stuffed animal. You'll also need a change of clothes for the day you go home. You probably won't need your pajamas. The hospital has special pajamas called hospital gowns for patients. Hospital gowns are comfortable. They are also easier to put on and take off than regular pajamas.

◀ Bringing your own toothbrush, toys, and stuffed animals will make you feel more comfortable in the hospital.

When You First Get There

The first thing you do when you get to a hospital is check in. Your parents will have to sign some papers. They do this in the waiting room. Most waiting rooms have toys to play with and magazines to look at.

Next, a nurse will help you put on your **ID bracelet** (EYE DEE BRAYS-let). An ID bracelet is a name tag that you wear on your wrist. It tells doctors and nurses who you are and why you're in the hospital.

It is important that you don't take your ID bracelet off until you go home. ▶

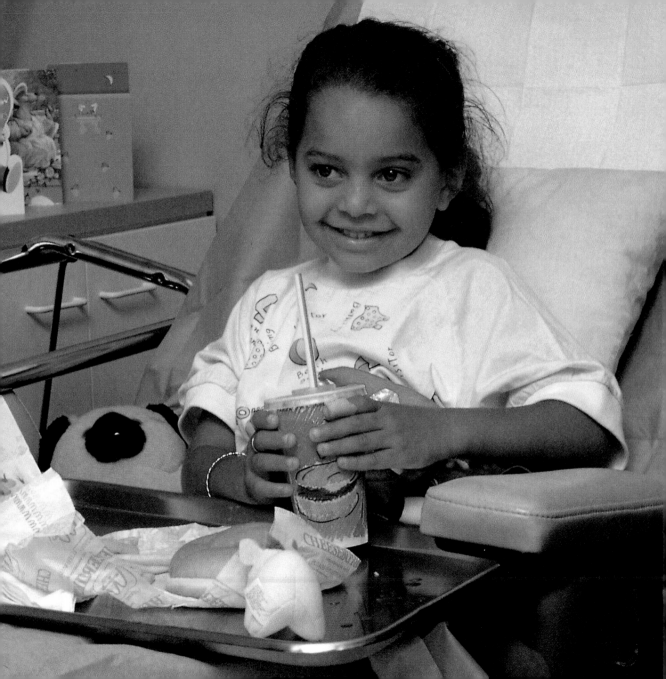

Eating at the Hospital

One fun thing you can do in a hospital is eat in bed. Hospital rooms have special trays that go across your lap. That way, you don't even have to get out of bed to eat. A hospital worker will bring you your meals three times a day.

◀ Sometimes your mom or dad can bring you your favorite foods for a special meal.

All Those Tubes!

In the hospital, your body may need help getting enough water and sugar to help you get better. The best way to get this is through an IV, or **intravenous** (IN-tra-VEE-nus) drip. An IV drip works like this: A tube is hooked up to a bag of water and sugar. It is also hooked up to a needle that a nurse inserts into a **vein** (VAYN) in your arm. The water and sugar drip slowly into your blood through the tube. It may hurt a little at first. But after a while, you forget that it's even there.

If you are scared, ask the nurse to explain what she is going to do. ▶

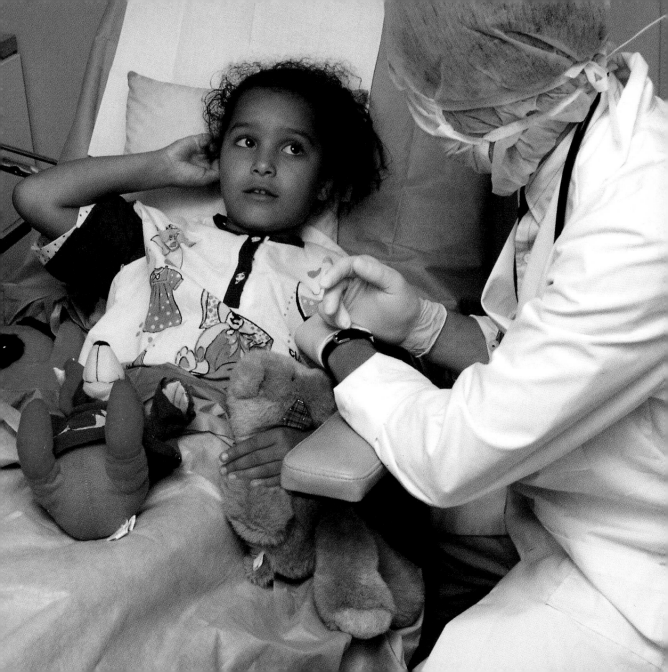

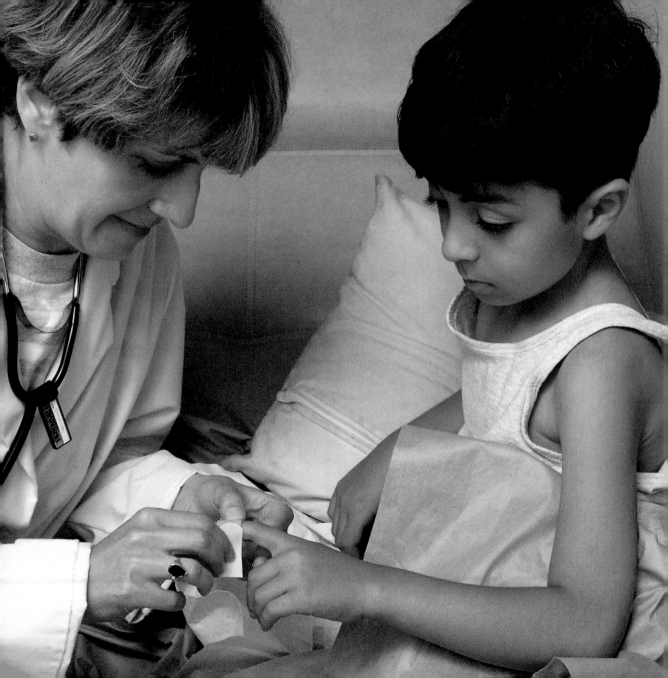

Different Kinds of Tests

Doctors have different ways of finding out what is making you sick. For example, a nurse may take a blood sample. She will do this by pricking your finger or arm with a needle. It hurts a little, but not a lot. Your finger or arm will stop bleeding quickly. Your body makes a lot of blood. It won't miss what the nurse took. You may have to have an X ray. An X-ray machine takes a picture of your insides. Doctors can look at the picture and see what's going on inside you. It doesn't hurt to have an X ray.

◀ It may sting a little when the nurse takes a blood sample, but it will stop hurting quickly.

Surgery

Sometimes the doctor has to work on the inside of your body. He may have to do **surgery** (SUR-jer-ee). You may have to have an **operation** (op-ur-AY-shun). Before the operation, a doctor will put a mask over your face. It has a special kind of gas flowing through it. This gas puts you to sleep so you won't feel the operation. You won't even remember what the doctor did. After the surgery, you will go to the recovery room. There you will rest until you wake up. Then a nurse will take you back to your hospital room.

Your parents will come see you as soon as you wake up after surgery. ▶

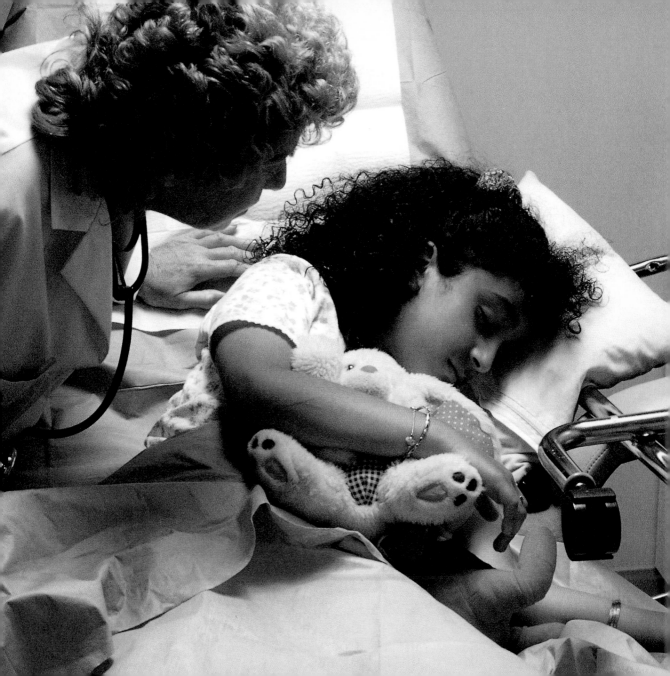

Where Are Mom and Dad?

Some hospitals let moms and dads stay with their kids overnight. Some have special rooms where moms and dads can sleep. Other hospitals don't let parents stay over. But they let parents come back first thing in the morning.

Whether your parents stay with you or not, there are doctors and nurses around all night long to make sure you're okay.

Someone will always be there to make sure you're okay.

Going Home

When your doctor says you're well enough, you can go home. The first thing you will do is change out of the hospital gown and put on your own clothes.

After you've packed all your things, a nurse will give you a ride in a wheelchair. She'll take you to the lobby of the hospital, where your parents can pick you up. Then you and your parents can all go home together, happy and healthy.

Glossary

healthy (HEL-thee) Having good health; not being sick or injured.

hospital (HOS-pih-tul) Place for the care of the sick or hurt.

ID bracelet (EYE DEE BRAYS-let) Name tag worn around the wrist that tells doctors and nurses who you are and why you are in the hospital.

intravenous (IN-tra-VEE-nus) Into a vein.

operation (op-ur-AY-shun) A way to fix diseases and injuries by surgery.

patient (PAY-shint) Person who is being treated by a doctor.

surgery (SUR-jer-ee) A way to treat sicknesses or hurt body parts by operations.

vein (VAYN) Tube in your body that blood flows through.

Index

MAI

11-15-98

GAYLORD FG